Little Book of Angelic Wisdom

Affirmations of Love, Healing, Hope, and Faith for Renewal of Heart, Spirit and Soul

Fran Lenzo

Minuteman Press • Melville, NY

Also by Fran Lenzo

"Angel Messages from Above"
Stories, Poems, Essays and
Loving Words from
John, My Guardian Angel

This "little book" is dedicated to my husband Jerry, who from the beginning has been open in heart and mind to the "advancement of angel consciousness,"

To my son, James, who, through his innocence and the challenges he has faced since birth, has taught me more about the meaning of unconditional love than any other person I know, and

To the many people who, through our spiritual healing workshops, have become our friends and joined us on our spiritual journey. Each person has brought a beam of light to our gatherings, and together we have grown in friendship, knowledge, understanding and God's love.

To all of God's messengers we so lovingly call "angel," thank you for your gentle guidance, common sense and humor which has helped us live our lives with a more positive and clear outlook.

I especially want to thank God, our Guiding Light, for bringing me Angel John, without whom there would be no words to put down on paper.

First edition March, 1996

For further information, and for correspondence to
the author, please contact

Angel Guidance, Inc.
POB 1560, Melville, NY 11747
or
E-mail: angelj94k@aol.com

ISBN:0-9644821-1-8

Library of Congress Catalog Card Number: 96-90647

Printed in the United States of America by
Minuteman Press, Melville, New York

Angel John's
Little Book of Angelic Wisdom

Affirmations of
Love, Healing,
Hope, and Faith
for Renewal of
Heart, Spirit and Soul

Fran Lenzo

Allow
my presence
to be
part of
your day,
and I will
present to you
gifts of
strength,
courage
and
love.

The Heavens
are here for you
at all times
to cover you with
the tenderness of
my love for you.
You need only look
within and above
to know this
divine wisdom.

1

I know there are angels all around me. They leave little hints all over the place. And then there are the times when they talk to me, and I'm not sure what I'm hearing. The words are always funny and kind, the visions are always divine. I feel sad for those who might wonder and doubt. With all of my angels around me, one thing I don't do is pout!

2

Dear Lord, I know I'm getting on in years. My eyesight is not as sharp, and I don't hear everything like I used to. Yet I believe this is your gift to me because I have had to look inside myself to see more clearly my direction and hear more accurately my lessons. Sometimes having less is having more.

3

I will not let that scale overpower me. I will not let that scale overpower me. I will not let that scale overpower me.

Please accept
my love for you
which is
abounding and pure.
It is through
your acceptance
that I am able
to be
your Father.

The older I get, the more I learn about myself and the less confused I become. Ah, wisdom of the ages!

I value me the way my friends and family value me. We never discount each other's feelings, and we use our "bargaining" powers to come to compromises that make us all winners.

I have a great recipe for my life: Take my intelligence, add positive thoughts and feelings about myself, stir in God's love, balanced emotions, humor, healthy food and physical exercise. Sit in quiet meditation to blend all ingredients. I have just created a masterpiece known as "me."

My life is like a yo-yo — up and down, up and down, loop de loop — Everything will be just fine as long as my string doesn't break!

My child,
I sit in love for you
as I watch your growth
of love of self.
This tells me
you are learning
the lessons which
I present to you
with open heart
and true belief.

🦋   There is no ending to my life. I will continue on and on into eternity to learn all that God wants me to learn. [8]

🦋   Why is it as I'm changing more and more, people around me understand me less and less? Maybe I need to explain it to them. [9]

🦋   I give myself the same patience to learn a new lesson as I give to someone I am teaching. [10]

🦋   The next time I expect someone to behave or react in a certain way and they don't, I will remember to be surprised but not disappointed or upset. [11]

The Heavens
are always ready
to receive you,
and I stand here
with open arms
and love
to welcome
my child
home.

[12] I finally understand what it means to pray...just talk to God like a friend. I can even shout and pout. He allows me my own pity party and waits with open arms to love me.

[13] When I lay my head down on my pillow at night, I will reflect on my day and say, "Thank You" to God and me for all that I have learned.

[14] Yes, it is a sunny day. I know the skies are cloudy and the weatherman says rain, yet I see the sun and God above the clouds to brighten my way.

[15] I am able to do all I desire in this lifetime. My time is my own, my goals set with success in mind, and "failure" is a word not in my life dictionary.

Have faith, my child,
when you feel
I have deserted you
and the days look
dark and bleak.
It is at those times
I am the closest to you.
Look beyond the fears
and worries
that blind you
and recognize
my presence.

16

I look at where I have been and am amazed.
I look at where I am now and am pleased.
I look at where I am going and I wonder.

17

Today I need to love me a lot, as much as
I can so I can face whatever comes my
way....Repeat after me....Today I need to love
me a lot, as much as I can so I can face
whatever comes my way...Repeat after me...

18

Sometimes I feel like there is no hope,
and then I'll see a small child wheeling her
chair with determination and a smile on her
face, or an elderly person walking proudly, cane
in hand, and I realize that "hope" is truly a
state of mind.

Forgive me,
my child,
for the disappointments
you may feel
when you think
I have not
heard your pleas.
My response is
always one of clarity.
I ask you to
see the answers
from a different view.

19

The acceptance of God in my life is non-negotiable. Family and friends are.

20

If I can keep one thing in mind that will help me get through rough times, it's that the hand of God is always lifting me up under my elbow and gently pushing me forward through the tunnel toward the light.

21

Dear God, please let me make friends with the food I eat today. Let me invite into my home only those "friends" which are healthy for my body, mind and soul. Those friends which make me feel good about me. And God, please let me be wise enough to know who my true "friends" are!

When you act upon
my teachings of
non-judgement and
compassion
for those
different than
yourself.
you act on truths
which are taught
for the love of
all my children.

22

As I sit in quiet solitude reflecting on my life, I will remember to be thankful for the quiet solitude when I can reflect on my life.

23

My friends reflect where I am in my life. Some friends may come and go, others have been with me since the beginning. This only means that my life is changing and constant at the same time.

24

I will never give up on myself. If God can believe in me, so can I. It's a great feeling knowing as I strive for a "better" me, He still loves the me I am today.

25

God has an open-door policy. He leaves the door open and I can go in anytime I want. He doesn't even need advance notice!

My child,
allow this day
to be a gift
from me to you.
May it be
experienced
and
enjoyed
one hour
at a time.

26 I look for my strength in my own heart, my own history, my own character. I have created myself through my experiences, and my experiences are profound.

27 When I need to understand the "whys" of my life, I only need to look inside myself. Then it's up to me to put the "whens" into action so I can make the necessary changes.

28 I lift myself up to the skies as I think about all the challenges I have successfully met and the work I have done to make me who I am today. I really LOVE ME!

29 When I feel low, I make every effort to tell myself about all the good parts of my life. It's not always easy to keep a "positive" attitude, yet the more I talk, the more I listen, the more I believe, the better I feel.

I hold you close
to my heart,
dear one.
I hold you close
to envelope you with
love
and
compassion.
Do the same for others,
and you will be given
eternal life.

🐝 I want IT now! I don't know what IT is yet, but I'll know IT when I see IT! That's what clear vision is all about.

🐝 The next time someone asks me for a favor, I will say "yes" immediately knowing that extending myself to them is my way of extending God's love to them.

🐝 When I'm bored, it only means I haven't taken the time to look around to see how I can help someone.

🐝 As I sit in traffic, I can either be upset, anxious and annoyed, or I can have a conversation with my angel, who always makes me laugh. And for the driver in the next car who is looking at me strangely, I just hold up my car phone and smile.

Listen,
hear me speak
of your lessons.
Listen,
hear me speak
of your courage.
All as one,
and
all for
my love
of you.

34

Sometimes I choose not to follow the wisdom that is within my heart. I guess that's what "learning the hard way" means.

35

Lord, let me be wise enough to give myself the same understanding and love I give to my family and friends.

36

I can look at my life as a comedy show when I see how many times I have taken pratfalls trying to get to my next level of "understanding."

37

God is my chiropractor for life — He makes enough adjustments to keep my mind straight with clear thinking and my back strong to carry my challenges easily.

Thank you
for bringing me
into your heart.
Your acceptance
of me
fills me with
elation and joy.
Your acceptance
of me
is all I need
to be fulfilled.

38

The Universe is a very big place with many nooks and crannies. I play the adventurer and travel each day to a part of it never known to me before.

39

Sometimes as I'm waiting for my ship to come in, I look out into the vast ocean and see a colorful rainbow in the sky. Taking the time to watch my rainbows helps my ship to come closer faster.

40

Balance in my life is brought to me through God by allowing His hand to touch my scale of life to keep me in check!

41

Happiness to me is being at peace with all my decisions, knowing I have gone deep within my mind, heart and soul before taking any action. The more I follow this principle, the happier I become.

Do not put aside
those who would
question your
belief in me.
I appear
in many
different ways,
and
as you know me,
you know
your own truth.

42

My life is like a flower garden with each year gently planted next to the previous ones to be nurtured as a whole. My garden continues to bloom each year with new flowers, new growth, a new me. I tend to my garden with tears of happiness and sadness, nutrients of positive affirmations, God's sunlight, and by removing all the weeds, no matter how deep they go. I enjoy being my own gardener.

43

Home, sweet home. My home is my refuge, my place of rest, where I can be me. I thank God for the warmth I feel as I enter my front door on a cold winter's day. To feel this warmth is to appreciate this gift from God.

44

When I look around and see all that Mother Nature has provided, my heart fills with love and appreciation. She is life and through her I live. She has fed me, clothed me, kept me protected. My thanks to her is my respect for all that she provides.

I am a gentle Father,
not to be feared.
I am a gentle Father,
here to remind you
of the wisdom you hold
within your heart.
Accept these words
as your truth and
your actions
will reflect
my teaching and
guidance.

45

I smile at life even on those dark and dreary days. I know my smile will be a sunbeam to someone in pain. I receive much pleasure in giving "light."

46

Songs will give me many messages of healing. I have to remember to keep the volume down so that only I hear the words.

47

I must remember that the times when I think everything is going wrong are the times when God is preparing me to enjoy the times when everything is going right!

48

As I go through my day, I must remember that everyone I meet at one time was an infant in a crib. Each of us had the same beginning, yet each of us has had many different experiences. This is what makes each of us special.

My child,
honor the differences
of others,
for it is in this
you have
the most in common.
As you judge another,
so do you judge me.

49 I love everybody around me - no matter how hard they try to ignore me!

50 I know I'm OK when I can take the daggers of negative words someone throws at me and change them into rays of sunshine.

51 Laughter from my tummy brings healing to my soul.

52 I know this illness has brought me fear and distress, yet my strength is coming from my belief in God's love for me. I focus His love on my pain, and I experience a healing of body, mind and spirit. As I accept this belief, it becomes my truth.

My child,
do not cry tears
of sadness, anger
or bitterness
for a loved one
who has come home to me.
They have not left you,
for they are by my side
and always with me.
Know as you feel
my presence,
you feel theirs.

53

I have a best friend. One who never lets me down. One who stands by me when others toss me aside. This friend is my guide and constant companion, listening quietly to my tales of woe, yet always making me feel I'm the most important person in the world. He is the best friend for everyone....all we need do is talk to Him....He's always there.

54

If I can look at a person who just upset me and remember he has God within him, I am a better person. But why are some people able to hide God so well?

55

Waiting for others to help me find myself is like waiting for a bus that's on a different schedule than mine...I'll never get to my destination!

Child, have patience
for the gifts
you want the most.
I present them to you
for your growth
in the
most appropriate way
and at the
most appropriate time.

56 When someone tells me they are miserable and they speak with negative words, I know this is my opportunity to help God bring them some light through the positive words I speak in return.

57 I follow my dreams by seeking my goals using my heart.

58 When my life becomes overwhelming and I don't think I can handle another crises, I call in the "Big Guy," and before I know it, everything falls into place. Why do I always wait until the last minute?

59 Today is a new day for me. Yes indeed, another day to find out a new fact about my life. Oh, to learn...Oh, to grow...Oh, to be me...Oh, to let my love flow. Enough poetry! Now on to real life. May whatever I learn today fill in a blank!

My love for you.
my child.
is greater
than the
oceans.
the skies.
the universe.
My love for you is
far beyond
your comprehension.
It is constant.

60 My life is mine to be happy, to be upset, to be determined, to be sad, to be thin, to be fat, to be up, to be down. My life is mine. I own it. I decide how I want to live. Boy, do I have a lot of decisions to make!

61 I give myself a bouquet of flowers every morning. They are the kind words I speak about myself, and the scent stays with me as I go through my day.

62 Each time I look at a newborn baby, a bud blooming into a flower of color and scent, a loaf of fresh-baked bread, I am reminded that each day is a new beginning for me. With the help of God and my own abilities, I can create my life any way I desire.

Listen to your heart,
my little one,
for the gentle words
you hear
will be
gifts of love,
understanding
and
compassion from
your
Father.

63

My life is like a balloon. Sometimes I'm filled with the helium of life, lifting me to the skies. And then there's that darn bird I run into who lets the air out and sends me back to Earth.

64

Sometimes what I worry about the most is a matter of my own creation and not really truth. I will look at the reality before adding the worry.

65

When I think too far ahead, my head fills with a puzzle that has pieces missing. Patience is the one piece that will fill in all the blanks.

66

I do believe in me....I do believe in me....I do believe in me...Yes, that _does_ sound right!

I ask you
to accept me as a
presence in your life.
It is
through this acceptance
of me that
you are accepting
of your
own gifts.

🐝 **67** I want to help people in any way I can. But first I have to help me. But then, if I help others, I _am_ helping me!

🐝 **68** Cliche — Live my life one day at a time. Truth — It works.

🐝 **69** There are those times when being alone is my gift to myself — No one to judge me, to question me, to observe or to comment. Now, <u>that's</u> a miracle!

🐝 **70** Each time I stand up for my rights with quiet conviction and a true belief in my value, I become stronger about who I am and what I am all about.

I watch over you,
my child,
in all ways.
My care is permanent
and all-encompassing.
My eyes are filled
with tears of joy
as you come closer
to me.

🐝 Why is it that many times I really do know all the answers, yet I have to ask my friends for their opinions first before I'm able to believe in mine?

🐝 My belief in me is greater than my chances of winning the lottery. If I take a chance on me, I know I will be a winner because I hold all the tickets!

🐝 My feelings about myself are determined not by the words, actions, opinions, ideas, feelings or statements of others. They are determined by me.

🐝 Even though there are some people in my life who choose to look at its cynical side, I will learn from them how to look for the positive side of life. For this I thank them.

I love you,
my child,
with a heart that
spans eternities.
I love you,
my child,
with a heart that
is created
only for you.

75

Sitting quietly with my close friends in conversation is often the time I can appreciate the loving differences we make in each other's lives.

76

My angel carries a "God" flashlight for those nights when we lose our power. God's energy is sure better than that bunny's because it's been going on and on for eons of time.

77

I work hard each day to reach a goal I will set for myself. I take the time to review this goal every so often to be sure it is still the direction I want to go. I always have the freedom to make any change I feel is necessary to fulfill my life's purpose.

78

I choose life because life is what gives me the greatest opportunities to know me.

I say to you my child,
my love for you
is
greater than
any other.
Accept this love
and
you will know
peace
and joy.

79

I want some old toys to play with. I want to sit with my crayons and building blocks again. I want my dollhouse, my cowboy outfit, my ballet shoes. I want to go back to my childhood so I can remember how to laugh, play, and observe what brought me to today.

80

I give thanks to those people who enjoyed telling me all the things that were wrong with me. They helped me to see my right side!

81

I know there's a light at the end of the tunnel, yet I wonder if I were to work on myself hard enough, might I be able to raise the wattage and see it sooner?

82

God sits on my right side and on my left side. In fact, God sits all around me and sits inside my heart and soul. My knowing this truth will always surround me in His light.

Love is what
I present to you.
Understand there are
no conditions
attached to it.
It is pure
and
it is yours.

83

When I feel like I'm on a roll, I won't let anyone stop my forward motion.

84

Sit down, stand up, run here, run there. Never stopping, always moving. I am powered by my will to do what I need to do and get to where I need to go. I only have to remember to fill my body with premium fuel, get a tune-up now and then, and have a wheel alignment so I can move with balance.

85

Sometimes I feel like a Thanksgiving turkey because all of the "stuffing" I've done. Yet, as I release it to the Universe, I know I'll reach my wishbone!

86

I can be in a relationship and at times still feel single. Those are the times I get to see myself in my own light.

My gift
to you each day
is the gift of knowing
my love for you is
an eternal flame
which can never
be dampened
by your denial
of me.

87

Did I forget to turn out the lights? Oh, no, that's my angel sitting by my door. It's such a relief knowing he's doing the "knight" shift.

88

It is very important for me to acknowledge what I have learned, what I want to learn and how I plan to learn. All of this leads me to who I am, where I am going and the purpose of my life. A masterpiece in progress!

89

I wonder how long it will take me to "find my way" if I call on God to create my roadmap?

90

Lord, as I go through a dark tunnel in my life, please be at the other end with your light so I can see my way clearly.

My light
is always around you,
dear one.
Know these words
as your truth
and you will always
feel the warmth
of my love.

91

Sometimes the only answer is time. Sometimes the only answer is a mystery.

92

I give myself time. Time to sit in silence, time to be alone, time to find humor, and time to talk on the phone!

93

I allow myself my mistakes each day because they are my greatest lessons. Dear God, please let me be wise enough so that each mistake is a new one and not a repeat performance!

94

Every day I bring myself closer to knowing who I am and what my purpose is for this lifetime. It's all a matter of asking the right questions, listening really closely to the answers I hear, and then acting upon my own advice.

As you welcome me
into your life,
my child,
I thank you
for your acceptance
of my
eternal love
for you.

95 I sometimes have a hard time seeing the flowers from the trees. But the scenery is so beautiful, I really don't mind!

96 This year is mine to do what I want, to make the changes I desire, to reach the goals I set, to laugh gently at my mistakes and to learn my truths.

97 I always have my own power to do what is needed for my growth. Now, I only need to remember to start my engine!

98 My intelligence is strong enough to lead me in the right direction. To feel with my heart and think with my mind is a perfect combination to help me reach my destination.

My little one,
I follow you
into eternity
to give you
comfort,
love,
hope,
peace
and
serenity.

99 I lift the spirits of those around me because I remember those times they lifted mine.

100 Now is the time for me to help a stranger find his way. In doing this I help myself to see what I need to learn.

101 When I demand, order and debate, I only create havoc in my life. When I request, ask, compromise and smile, I create my life according to my desires.

102 The seat of judgement can be hard and unyielding. Rather than judge another, I prefer sitting on a loveseat, observing humanity with an open mind and heart.

Have faith
in me child.
for your Father
does know
what is
best for you.
My teachings are
always
of love.

103

I can learn anything I put my mind to. Believing this is true is the first part. Acting upon my belief is the second.

104

Today is a new beginning for me. A chance to make adjustments and a chance to love myself in the process.

105

Being prepared for the future means I only have to handle what comes my way today.

106

My sense of who I am changes every so often. As I go through different experiences, as I accept new ideas and thinking, I find myself evolving and growing. And, having God in my life is the one experience which keeps me balanced and centered as I go through the others.

Feel love and compassion
in your heart
for those who have
given you pain.
It is through
this action
you do my bidding
and receive
love which is
unconditional.

107

I give myself a pat on my back for good behavior...now I'll do something daring and different!

108

My physical body needs to be changed to reflect my feelings about myself, yet if I remember that I'm loved just the way I am, I won't have to break a sweat!

109

Sometimes it seems the harder I work to create my life exactly the way I want it, there are more people who make it more difficult for me to reach my goals. I can choose to work around them or to stomp on them. I think God would prefer I do the first because the second would make a mess of my shoes!

Patience, my child,
is a very special gift
I give to you.
It is through
your acceptance
of patience
you will see
your life unfold
in magnitude
great
and
profound.

110 "Finding" myself only matters if I truly feel lost. I wonder if God has a "Lost and Found" Department?

111 When I listen closely to my heart, I feel my spirits lifting me to the heavens because I know I have followed my own truth.

112 I can reach my own Superbowl of Life as long as I'm the Coach, Captain and Waterboy of my own team.

113 Dear Lord, let me take the time to really listen when someone else is speaking instead of planning what I will say next. This way I won't miss the compliments I might be given!

My messages
to my child
are many times
so gentle
they are not
heard clearly.
I ask you to sit
in silent contemplation
and the messages
will be profound.

114

My life can be more difficult, more beautiful, more enjoyable, more disasterous. The more I think about it, the more I see my power to choose.

115

I never say, "No Way!" That usually means the Universe will respond with "You Wanna Bet?"

116

The way I see it, the more I give my "power" to God to help me with my life, the more light I receive from Him. A wonderful exchange!

117

Heaven is a place where I am at peace and feel God's love. I realize that Heaven is here on Earth because I feel his presence within me. As I accept God close to my heart, I accept my place in heaven.

As you walk
through your day,
I offer
my hand to guide you,
my heart to love you,
my teachings
to educate you,
and
my joy
to share
with you.

118
Being alone is not the same as being lonely. With the first, I enjoy my own company. With the second, I forgot to invite myself in.

119
Today is the day that begins my life anew. A new chance to discover more about the me I've never known and to be pleased in the process.

120
This is the year I will take the bull by the horns, toss him to the ground, sit on his back and ride him to my destination.

121
God is the best health provider I can have because He takes care of my life for an eternity and the only premium I pay is my belief in His love for me.

I am with you
even as your life
is filled with
the responsibilities
of living
and
you are not aware
of my
presence.
Rest easy
knowing this truth.

122 True family are those people who let me be me and still say, "You're OK!"

123 I choose to be with people who will elevate my mind, my spirit, my life. I choose to do the same for them, and we all grow from the experience.

124 At those times when things don't go my way, I have to remember that this is only another lesson sent to me from the heavens, and sometimes there are clouds in that big blue sky.

125 Even though I don't see my angel, I know he's around. He's the one who helps me open that "child proof" bottle, find my keys and who opens my eyes to all those unexpected "coincidences" of my life. He's my "unseen" hero.

The tears
of sadness that gently
roll down your cheek
are my healing presence
in your life.
Together let us allow
our tears
to close
the wounds
of your heart.

126

I am given many challenges and opportunities to grow. Some are more painful than others, and I do appreciate the "time-outs" when nothing is happening.

127

To look deep inside myself can sometimes bring me pain. But the wisdom I gain brings me love of myself which is divine.

128

A surprise is when the Universe provides me with a well-deserved treat. And it doesn't mean extra calories!

129

I love myself enough to forgive me for loving myself too much.

The times
of trouble
when you think
I am not with you
are the times
my presence
is the strongest.
I ask you to believe
these words and
you will
experience truth.

130

I look to my friends for comfort, honesty and support. They never let me down, they only lift me up.

131

I will look in my mirror each morning and smile at the reflection I see. If God can love me the way I am, who am I to disagree?

132

Sometimes I cry in sadness about the way I've lived my life and the choices I have made. But then there are the times when I smile in happiness because I will have made the changes needed to take away the sadness.

133

One piece of cake means another hour on the treadmill. On the other hand, eating a carrot stick means no movement on my part. Maybe if I eat carrot cake I can compromise and walk half an hour.

I ask you
to give yourself
to those around you
in need.
In return
you will receive
my loving light
which surrounds you
in protection
and
warmth.

134

My life is mine to create, mine to design. But, how many times have I given <u>my</u> crayons to someone else to make <u>my</u> pictures, and they don't even use the colors I like?

135

Laugh, laugh, laugh — Life sure gives me a lot to laugh about, yet I sometimes have to laugh through my tears.

136

It is possible for this day to go exactly as I want it. I just need to check in with God in the morning to be sure we both have the same game plan.

137

Sometimes I hear a song that brings back a happy memory. Sometimes the memory will be sad. In either case I can see my life's musical played out before me which helps me to stay in tune with the flow of the Universe.

Be at peace, my child.
Know the challenges
of each day
are presented as
your lessons for
your lifetime.
As each one is learned,
the challenge
of the lesson
is diminished
and you are stronger
for the learning.

138

As I walk through my workday, I make a conscious effort to find one pleasant event within each hour. When it's time to go home, I will have many enjoyable memories to take with me.

139

I can be as strong as I need to be. All I have to do is say these words enough times for me to realize this is true.

140

If I wait long enough, I know the Universe will provide me with everything I desire. Or is that need? Hopefully, whatever I need will be my desire so the Universe will have an easy time providing.

141

I love January 1 of each year. It means a new beginning, a new chance to become a new me, which means I can open new charge accounts under my new name.

My child,
you may question
my actions
and wonder why.
As you sit in
quiet reflection
to hear my answers,
you will reach a state of
understanding and
acceptance from the
center of your heart.

142

I allow my friends into my life to give me support and love. I do the same in return, and we create a true family.

143

I plant my garden every day. Now all I need is miracle grow!

144

Lord, I know you are my teacher, and school is open twenty-four hours a day, yet there are those times when a recess would be appreciated.

145

Now is the time for me to help a stranger find his way. In doing this, I help myself to see what _I_ need to learn.

Listen to your heart,
my little one,
for the gentle words
you hear will be a
gift from your Father.
Let them touch your
heart and soul
to bring you to a
place of love,
peace and serenity.

146

When everything seems hopeless, and I'm not sure which way to turn, all I need do is STOP long enough to hear this refrain: "You are my child, and I love you so. Please allow me to guide you to where you need to go". When I STOP, LISTEN and FOLLOW, it's only a matter of time for hopefulness to return.

147

My time is precious, dear Lord. Please help me to spend it wisely, with love and with a goal in mind. And then let me have those few moments each day when my wisdom rests and I sit quietly in reflection.

148

When someone tells me something about me for "my own good," I'll be courteous and listen with an open heart and open mind, say "thank you" with a feeling of love, and then do what <u>I</u> know is best for me.

I present
to you
eternal life,
for in eternal life
my gifts of love
to you
continue into
eternity.

149

I need to be more patient with myself. When I'm in a hurry, I find myself skipping important steps.

150

I need to have more patience with my "teachers." They have a hard enough time with their "student."

151

As I sit in quiet contemplation of my life, I realize that everything _is_ going my way. I just have to find out where my way is leading me!

152

I know that if I'm patient, in time, all the questions I ask will be answered by God. Boy, wouldn't it be great if He would deliver in an hour, just like the pizza parlor?!

I say to you,
my teachings are
always of love,
understanding,
non-judgement and
forgiveness.
As you present
my teachings
to your neighbors,
you truly know me.

153

Why is it I always ask for help when I feel the most vulnerable? Maybe I need to look inside myself for my strength - especially at those times when no one else is around, and all I have is me.

154

The question is not, "Why did he do that to me?" The question is, "Why am I responding this way?" The answer will come from within.

155

I'll never underestimate God's presence in my life. He surprises me every day with little gifts of love, hope and faith. And I do love to open those packages!

156

I love me enough to change those things about me I'm not happy with. In the meantime I'll love me just the way I am.

'Be patient
with yourself.
my child.
for it is in
your practice
of patience that
the gifts received
are appreciated
the most.

157

My life flows like the rivers, but every so often I run into a dam. Then I have to work like a beaver to get over and get through. And I'm worth it!

158

There are those times when I love having people around me. And then there are those times when I love being alone. Being human means being social and solitary. Being human means me being me.

159

Sometimes I wonder what my life is all about. Why I'm here. Where I'm going. Why certain people are in my life. I wonder if God would be willing to play "20 Questions" with me so I can get some answers?

As you
read these words,
know I am
by your side,
ready to
take your hand
to guide you
to a
love of
yourself.

160 I accept everything I'm given, no matter how upsetting. I can do this because I recognize God is nearby, ready to help.

161 Sticks and stones can break my bones and mean words can break my heart. As I remember this pain, may I never inflict on someone else the same.

162 God, I know you hear everything I say and watch everything I do. Is there a way that I can see and hear you too? OK, OK, I understand — everything that happens to me is touched by your hand.

163 My success in this lifetime isn't based on how much money I make. It's based on how many people I affect in a positive way. After all, Heaven doesn't have savings accounts, but I know God watches how many kindness deposits I make into my lifetime account.

My love
for you, child,
is of permanence,
always within,
above and
around you.
As you understand
and accept these words
as your truth,
your pain is diminished.

164

There is no reason on this Earth that I cannot achieve any goal I set for myself. The important thing to remember is that I'm the only one who decides what my goal is, and I'm the only reason I wouldn't reach it.

165

This morning I'll sing a happy tune, one which makes me smile. Or maybe I'll say a few kind words to myself, ones that will lift me off the floor. Or maybe I'll just sit for a few moments and reflect on all the good things in my life. No matter what I choose to do, it will bring me to loving myself. And that's the best gift I can give me!

166

To those people who want to make me crazy by their constant requests for me to change who I am to fit their needs, I relinquish your hold over me and say "Thank you" for helping me find my own strength.

My little one,
as you feel
your strength
as you face
your challenges,
you are feeling
my love
for you.

167

I'm as young and open to love as on the day I was born. The only difference is now I'm potty trained and can feed myself.

168

Lord, help me through the days that are filled with decisions, challenges and heartaches. Please guide me and let me feel your presence, for through your gifts to me, I will handle each hour with calmness and serenity.

169

Dear Lord, let me be wise enough to turn to my friends for comfort and support when I'm in pain, and wise enough to know when they have heard enough.

170

Ah, life is such a mystery. I never know what will happen next. But then, do I really want to know what to expect? I need to think about that one.

My lessons for you
may seem harsh.
yet as you
go through each one
you have added another
source of strength
to your being.
And that source is
you.

If you would like to order additional copies of *Angel John's Little Book of Angelic Wisdom* or *Angel Messages from Above*, please fill out the order form on the next page, include your check or money order, made out to **Angel Guidance**, and mail it to:

Angel Guidance, Inc.
POB 1560
Melville, NY 11747

When you order a copy of *Angel Messages from Above*, Angel John will inscribe a personal message on the inside front cover as well as give you the name of one of your angels. Please be sure to tell us the name of the person for whom the book is intended.

You may also use the order form to put your name on our mailing list to receive *The Angel John Express* newsletter, at no charge, which is published four times a year.

Angel Guidance Inc.

POB 1560, Melville, NY 11747

Order by Phone with Visa/Mastercard
1-800-265-6626

Please make checks/money orders payable to Angel Guidance, Inc.

ORDER FORM

Please Print Your Name

Address

City   State   Zip

QTY

_____   *Angel John's Little Book* @ $7.00   _____

_____   *Angel Messages* @ $14.95   _____

SHIPPING TABLE

Up to $10 add	$3.00
$10 to $25 add	$4.50
$25 to $45 add	$5.50
Over $45 add	$6.50

**NY State residents add*
appropriate sales tax

Subtotal   _____

Shipping   _____

**Sales Tax   _____

Total $ _____

Name of person for whom book is intended:

☐YES, Please send me "The Angel John Express."

✗ 94 ✗